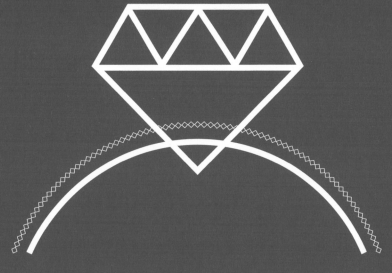

Will You Marry Me?

— Creative Wedding Planning & Design —

Will You Marry Me ?

Creative Wedding Planning & Design

©SendPoints Publishing Co., Ltd.

EDITED & PUBLISHED BY SendPoints Publishing Co., Ltd.

PUBLISHER: Lin Gengli

PUBLISHING DIRECTOR: Lin Shijian

EDITORIAL DIRECTOR: Sundae Li

EXECUTIVE EDITOR: Ellyse Ho, Huang Shaojun

ART DIRECTOR: He Wanling

EXECUTIVE ART EDITOR: He Wanling

PROOFREADING: Sundae Li

ADDRESS: Room 15A Block 9 Tsui Chuk Garden, Wong Tai Sin, Kowloon, Hong Kong

TEL: +852-35832323 / **FAX:** +852-35832448

EMAIL: info@sendpoints.cn

DISTRIBUTED BY Guangzhou SendPoints Book Co., Ltd.

SALES MANAGER: Zhang Juan (China), Sissi (International)

GUANGZHOU: +86-20-89095121

BEIJING: +86-10-84139071

SHANGHAI: +86-21-63523469

EMAIL: overseas01@sendpoints.cn

WEBSITE: www.sendpoints.cn

ISBN 978-988-13835-4-9

P006/ *Introduction*

P008/ *Wedding Ceremonies*

P192

Wedding
Elements

P254

Index

Introduction

By Isabel Smith

In the majority of the world's cultures, people choose partners for life—a person with whom to share a home, build a life, and raise children. The significance of this, the moment when these two people ceremoniously come together to form a new family tie has been celebrated and formalized in various ways since before ancient times.

Weddings and the celebrations that follow offer a unique opportunity for the uniting families to meet, share in the bonds of responsibility which come with the new legal connection, celebrate the union of the marrying pair and wish them well on their journey together. The reasons leading people to marry change little over time and across borders, but there is glorious variety amongst the ways in which a wedding is celebrated around the world with legal, religious and cultural factors coming in to play.

In today's modern, technology-driven world where traditions and trends from across the globe can be instantly shared. After all, this is the first era during which a wedding in Thailand can be filmed on a smartphone, uploaded to the web and immediately viewed by a bride planning her day in Iceland. There has been a shift, with a lot less focus on customs, and a lot more attention being paid to customization. Couples are increasingly looking to other countries and cultures for ideas on how to personalize their wedding and make the event a more unique reflection of them and their lives together.

This shift in focus has created the most wonderful forum for design in the wedding world; Traditional attire mixed with current fashion, unusual colours, patterns and textures combining to create unique themes, the latest entertainment ideas featuring during the customary drinks reception and both scripture and contemporary poetry appearing in multi-faith ceremonies.

Whilst one hopes that the significance of each wedding and its subsequent marriage are not lost on brides and grooms as they become swept up in the whirlwind of details we so love to consume, we also hope that this book will allow you to explore both the trends and traditions from around the world in an effort to inform and inspire.

Contents
Wedding Ceremonies

P012
ALL YOU NEED IS LOVE

P018
EMERALD 1970s WEDDING INSPIRATION

P022
HERITAGE WOODLAND OAK GROVE WEDDING

P028
CIRCUS THEME WEDDING

P034
TRADITIONAL CHINESE WEDDING

P038
BEN & PEISURE'S WEDDING

P044
LUCIA & FANIE'S WEDDING

P050
DESTINATION WEDDING: SONOMA CALIFORNIA

P056
BRYAN & SHANNON COMBEST'S WEDDING

P062
VINTAGE WEDDING IN LAXENBURG

P066
MALIBU VINEYARDS WEDDING

P072
TOMAS & TERESA'S WEDDING

P078
MORGAN & CHRIS'S WEDDING

P082
KATE SPADE WEDDING INSPIRATION

P088
THE POST-80s' WEDDING PARTY

P094
CALLI & CALEB'S NORTHWEST BEACH WEDDING

P102

Deric & Julia's Glamorous Seattle Wedding

P108

Brianne & Erik's Seattle Art Gallery
Wedding

P114

Gerard & Clara's Wedding

P120

A Canadian Fall Wedding

P126

Victoria & Kieron's Nostalgic Los Angeles
Wedding

P132

Elizabeth & Preston's Hip New York Farm
Wedding

P138

Helen & Steve's Wedding

P144

Joshua Tree Wedding

P150

Oregon Summer Wedding

P156

Brent & Cathy's Wedding

P164

Jenny & Nick's Wedding

P170

Jaymee & Reis's wedding

P176

Nathanael & Shannon Clanton's
Wedding

P186

Catherine & Robert's Wedding

ALL YOU NEED IS LOVE
The 70s; Beatles

Photographer   **Designer/Studio**   **Website**
Nadia Huerta   Sweet Sunday Events   junebugcompany.com   Dallas, TX, USA

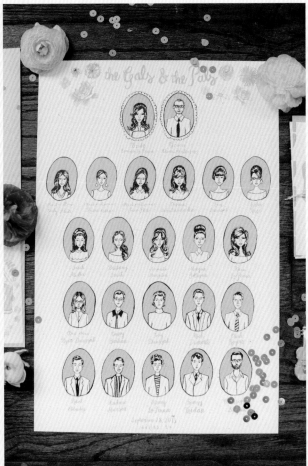

A 70's theme, 1,200 handmade paper flowers and the most fun and energetic couple and bridal party was led by a ceremony flawlessly set with mod and antique furniture placed in between white fur throw accented seating. An ombre polka dotted aisle runner created the perfect entrance for the wedding party all holding custom signs and tambourines. "All You Need Is Love" was the theme of the evening. The Stationery Bakery hand painted the 12 feet tall floral mural. Blossoming vines of pink and yellow paper flowers delicately hanged above the aisle, bringing the outdoors in and adding bright pops of color.

At the reception, mod tables with chrome legs lined either side of the dance floor and lounge area on the second floor. On them, rested a seamless mix of hand crafted floral runners, printed napkins, and glittery utensil bags. With the flowering vines hanging above each table and real flower arrangements full of ranunculus, tulips, and dahlias sitting below, a stunning color block effect covered the space. Sparkling gold chia pets, custom teal banquet seating, and mod white vases holding tapered candles and sequins were just a few more of the tidbits added to this space.

For the sendoff, biodegradable pink and purple confetti was tossed as the newlyweds jumped into a 70's VW van and headed off to start their new life. Carissa and Adam's wedding was bursting with beautiful details and fun design elements.

EMERALD 1970S WEDDING INSPIRATION
The 70's

Photographer
Jody Savage Photography

Designer/Studio
Simply Loves Wedding & Design

Website
simplyloves.com

Minnesota, USA

This wedding inspiration shoot integrated the groom's passion for classic cars with a soft and romantic touch of handmade objects and natural yarns. The designer created a 1970s wedding featured macramé details. To this end, a classic car appeared on the shoot venue of rough exterior while soft linens were used to decorate the table. The watercolor invitation cards added to the romance and sweetness of the joyful occasion.

HERITAGE WOODLAND OAK GROVE WEDDING
Rustic; Vintage

Photographer
Jasmine Fitzwilliam

Designer/Studio
Let's Frolic Together

Website
www.letsfrolictogether.com

Ramona, CA, USA

a condition of complete SIMPLICITY

MENU
Appetizer
• Ranchos House Salad

Entrée
• Lobster Tacos
• Carne Asada Tacos
• Chicken Enchiladas
• Avacado blue corn Enchiladas

Dessert
• organic vegan carrot
   cupcakes

This was not a wedding, but the tender and profound launch of a marriage. It rallies a community of friends and family, which connects people emotionally. Hidden Oaks in Ramona could not have proven to be a more perfect venue. Shading the families and friends from an incredibly intense sun, these grand oaks strung with lights wrapped everyone in a cozy wonder and a palpable joy. Heritage was their inspiration word, as they crafted a celebration that would feel timeless and tender. Delightfully historic collectibles and found vintage pieces were combined with some beautifully built tables and signage to create the perfect setting for their celebration.

Circus Theme Wedding
Retro-fun

Photographer
Kelsea Holder Photography

Designer/Studio
Taylor Made Events and Design

Website
www.taylormadeeventsanddesign.com

San Luis Obispo, CA, USA

Kelsea Holder Photography worked with Taylor Made Events and Design and A Little Birdie Told Me to design a handmade wedding at an early 20th century home, highlighted with a cigar girl, popcorn, and pinwheels. Flying Caballos Guest Ranch is the most beautiful and quirky venue tucked in the rolling hills of Edna Valley wine country, just outside downtown San Luis Obispo. This colorfully restored 1905 ranch house is any whimsy vintage couple's dream. This ultra-fun wedding features some unique twists such as pinwheel "bouquets" and was packed with good food and good entertainment. Guests can enjoy gourmet renditions of classics such as hot dogs and funnel cakes and spend the evening playing croquet or sipping some bubbly by the old milk truck drink stand.

TRADITIONAL CHINESE WEDDING

Vintage; Traditional Chinese

Photographer
Pin Vision & Li Yao

Designer/Studio
TOGETHER

Website
weibo.com/u/3234496314?topnav=1&wvr=6&topsug=1

Zhejiang Province, China

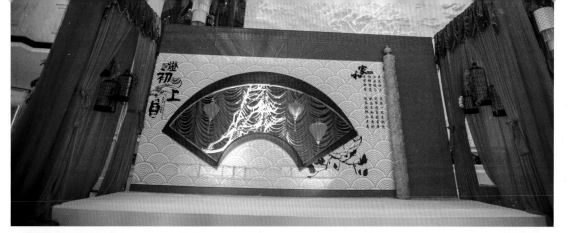

Red, the traditional Chinese wedding color that symbolizes luck, happiness and prosperity covered the whole wedding venue. The vintage wedding gown and hairdressing of the bride added to the festive joy of the occasion while offering a glimpse into the traditional wedding in ancient China. Red dates, peanuts, dried longan and lotus seeds carries the blessings of happy marriage and the hope for many offspring.

Ben & Peisure's Wedding

Pop; American comics

Photographer   **Designer/Studio**   **Website**

Hema   Swan Real Wedding   www.wedding-swan.com   Guangzhou, China

The Pop and American comics wedding style drew inspiration from the couple's shared interest in American movies and their love for adventures. The strong contrasting colors, a typical Pop feature symbolized the beautiful combination of the groom's calm personality and the bride's more cheerful and passionate nature. The orange and yellow and blue palette helped create an exciting wedding party vibe. The designer believes wedding ceremony has no fixed form and it is more about witnessing the vows the newlyweds make to each other. The DIY bridal bouquet made of fabric and lace was a good example of meanings triumphing forms. The bride doesn't like receiving fresh-cut flowers because she doesn't like seeing them withering, making the fabric bouquet a sweet and romantic touch in the wedding design.

The use of a large amount of colorful paper flowers added an emotional touch to the ceremony while helping the planner to keep the budget within range. For the table setting, a canvas-like fabric was chosen for the tablecloth with Pop style patterns printed on it, creating a consistent Pop style.

Lucia & Fanie's Wedding

DIY; Refreshing and fun

Photographer
Lad & Lass Wedding Photography

Designer/Studio
Lucia Vanzyl & Rosanna Duncan

Website
www.ladandlass.co.za

Melville, Johannesburg, South Africa

This is a beautifully planned DIY wedding created by the bride and her mother. With a limited budget they focused on the most important things to them, photographs and food. The bride had a clear idea of what she wanted in a wedding and what really excited her. Most of the décor was homemade along with the thank-you gifts. The refreshing plants and flowers, DIY table decorations were the lovely elements that made up a beautiful but simple wedding.

DESTINATION WEDDING: SONOMA CALIFORNIA

Romantic; Vintage

Photographer
Volatilephoto.com

Designer/Studio
Mandy Forlenza Sticos

Website
mandyforlenza.com

Sonoma, CA, USA

Ladies

A Memento

For Your Tears
Of Happiness

RUMIANO BROS.

I went to Turks and Caicos. I found a wife
thanks to Mandy Fortenza, George, welcome to
the club! My best thoughts and love to you
— RON ZGATZ

Mandy— thank you for everything! I'm so
happy you and George found each other!
Wishing you a life full of love, rich happiness
and fun!
♡ Jean

The concept for this intimate destination wedding was focused on romantic vintage details. Everything from the assorted vintage embroidered napkins to the polaroid guest book was carefully curated to create a "cozy at home" vibe while guests celebrated the union 2,500 miles from New York City.

BRYAN & SHANNON COMBEST'S Wedding

Fall; Rustic; Barn

Photographer
Nadia Huerta

Designer/Studio
Bryan & Shannon Combest (The couple)

Website
junebugcompany.com

Arlington, TX, USA

The bride's appreciation of historical antiquities from an early age influenced many of the wedding decisions. The venue was a historical barn with many fall colors and fallen leaves dancing around it. Fall is her favorite season of the year, so many of the decorations and wedding colors were based on the colors of fall leaves. Many of the table decorations had amber glassware, pumpkins, burlap, and old books that were collected during out yearlong engagement. The main wedding color was mustard yellow because it represented her grandmother's citrine necklace and earring set she wore that day. The goal was to make every aspect of the wedding personal to the couple so that the wedding was really a representation of their union.

VINTAGE WEDDING IN LAXENBURG

Vintage; Chic

Photographer
Thomas Steibl

Designer/Studio
Thomas Steibl, Ulrike Dorner & Georg Leditzky

Website
www.thomassteibl.com

Laxenburg, Austria

This wedding was the result of a terrific cooperation of many professionals. The garden wedding with a vintage flavor was held in the beautiful venue in Orangerie Laxenburg. The accessories and paper goods of Die SELLERIE fit just perfectly into this wedding. The arrangement of all the little details brought together a romantic reunion of love. Highlighting the couple's love of nature, a wide range of natural materials such as wood were used to add to the joy and liveliness of the occasion.

Georg

Malibu Vineyards Wedding

Organic; Farm-to-table; Family

Photographer
Leila Brewster Photography

Designer/Studio
Tiffany Bowne of Lounge Couture Inc.

Website
www.loungecouture.com

CA, USA

This is a wedding with a pleasant organic touch. In the Triumfo Creek Vineyards, the couple got married under the 200 year oak tree. Lilla Bello perfectly created the floral design with fresh cut, loose and airy flowers. The flowers were put in different sized vases to add to the "fresh cut" look. The colors were blush and in neutral tones. The couple wanted an evening with their close family and friends in an intimate setting. The flowers reflected a farm-to-table theme and the intimacy was brought to the table with the main course and sides served family style.

Global Cuisine created a delicious menu that was presented in a unique and tasteful way. The charcuterie station with fresh cheese and meat was a perfect casual intro into dinner. The "Vineyard Collection" provided by Town & Country Rentals added to the outdoor, rustic feel. The invitations were custom-made from Copper Willow and reflected the energy and look of the event.

TOMAS & TERESA'S WEDDING
Elegant; Branding; Family

Photographer
Gianluca & Mary Adovasio

Designer/Studio
Concreate Studio

Website
www.concreate.it

Rovigo, Italy

TOMAS+TERESA
21GIUGNO 2013

In this wedding, the groom wanted to realize an out-and-out brand that pivots on the shape of a tree. In the logo design, love is represented through two hearts, which take shape among the branches and the roots of the tree—the symbol of life, growth and communion. The theme was then reflected and developed in the whole wedding's visual identity: the invitations, the booklets of the Mass, the menu and in the place cards, and in the party favor—a bonsai. The black and white contrasting colors were applied throughout the wedding, resulting in a classic European elegant wedding.

MORGAN & CHRIS' WEDDING
Bold; Pop color

Photographer
Milou + Olin Photography

Designer/Studio
Yelena Johnson of the Stylish Soiree

Website
milouandolin.com

San Jose, CA, USA

The inspiration of this wedding came from Kate Spade's bold stripes, colors that pop and graphic details that are a perfect mix of modern feminine styles. The couple found their perfect venue—the Sainte Claire Hotel in the middle of downtown San Jose. Its authentic 1920s architectural details, glass-domed atrium, and beautiful chandelier-filled ballroom were ideal for an indoor ceremony and reception.

The bride wanted the special day to be more of a giant celebration or lavish party than a serious, formal affair. So she approached a team she could trust completely to create the special day. And obviously, the result proved to be great. They gifted the bride with an incredible bouquet and modern, stylish boutonnieres as well as a floral ceremony backdrop and beautiful centerpieces.

KATE SPADE WEDDING INSPIRATION
Bohemian Modern

Photographer
Danielle Poff Photography

Designer/Studio
Michaela Noelle Designs

Website
www.daniellepoff.com

Santa Barbara, CA, USA

The wedding features a bohemian sophistication with funky and natural elements. To provide a pleasant ambience for the guests in an afternoon wedding, the designer used teak wood tables, succulents and bright pink flowers. The wedding site, Santa Barbara Historical Museum, served as a perfect backdrop with its beautiful natural bricks, green ivy, cacti and flowers galore. The recipe of this amiable look is simple: clear glass plates with a patterned plate on top, bright flowers in a plain color vase, gold flatware, a variety of glassware and some colorful cacti for the table top. Some special elements for name card holder were used to please the guests, such as baby succulents. The bohemian style was show on the bride's gown and headpiece.

Sweets FROM THE Sweethearts

THE POST-80S' WEDDING PARTY
Vintage; Whimsical

Photographer
Tangvision

Designer/Studio
IMAGINE WEDDING

Website
www.imaginegroup.cn

Shanghai, China

The couple both belonged to the post-80s generation, a generation of Chinese people grew up in the middle of a clash between tradition and modern influences. They wanted a wedding that was fun and relaxing to celebrate a moment of joy when they and their guests were allowed to feel relaxed and at ease. An old wooden desk decorated with flowers and vases represents the refreshing elements that they longed for in a wedding. The orange and white lighted canopies placed at the entrance of the venue helped create a dreamy vintage setting for the wedding.

CALLI & CALEB'S NORTHWEST BEACH WEDDING

Nature & Beach

Photographer
Carina Skrobecki

Designer/Studio
Caleb Swenson (groom)

Website
www.carinaskrobecki.com

WA, USA

The couple wanted a whimsical and elegant wedding with the beauty of nature all around them—water, mountains, trees and beach. They had a great passion for nature and everything outdoors and spent a lot of time hiking, camping, and exploring, which they hoped could be reflected in the wedding. Alderbrook Lodge ended up being the best place for the wedding as it's nestled right along the water's edge on Hood Canal in Washington State. From the back lawn, you can see the beach, forests and mountains in one sweeping view.

The ceremony was held on the lawn overlooking the water, as well as the cocktail hour, and the reception took place underneath a large white tent. Each of the 26 dinner tables were individually designed by the couple, as well as family friends. In fact, all decoration and design work were done by them, which was what made the wedding day truly unique to them.

CABINS
FOR RENT

AND HAND IN HAND
ON THE EDGE OF
THE SAND, THEY
DANCED BY THE
LIGHT OF THE MOON

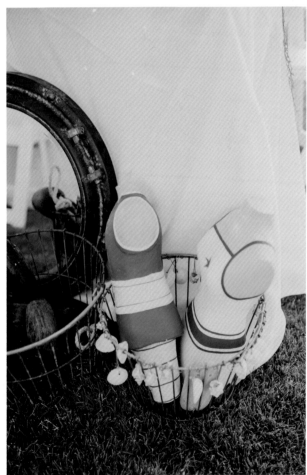

A mixture of pieces from pottery barn, friends home's, and handmade items were used at the wedding—each table had an eclectic mix of old beach signs, shells, netting, wooden seagulls, bottles and tiny string lighting to help capture the beachy feel. When the sun went down, the tables illuminated and made the large wedding feel smaller and more intimate.

Deric & Julia's Glamorous Seattle Wedding

Glamorous; Chic; Black Tie

Photographer
Carina Skrobecki

Designer/Studio
Julia (bride) & It's Your Day Event

Website
www.carinaskrobecki.com

Seattle, WA, USA

Please find your seats!

Table One
SUE LATENDRESSE
PHIL LATENDRESSE
CHELSEY PULLMAN
JORDAN PULLMAN
DOUG PULLMAN
JOHN LATENDRESSE
SUSIE LATENDRESSE

Table Two
KATHLEEN LARA
ROBERT KUCERA
JOE LARA
SONJA CRYSTAL
MARIA EMERSON
PATRICIA TURNER
NATALIE SAMFORD
JASEN SAMFORD

Table Three
VERA ORWOLL
OVE ORWOLL
DAVID ORWOLL
PENNIE ORWOLL
NINA ORWOLL

Table Four
CORINA KINGDON
SCOTT KINGDON
ANTON ASCHERL
ZULLAYLEE ASCHERL
TERESA ASCHERL
JOE ASCHERL

Table Five
MARTY LATENDRESSE
LYNNE LATENDRESSE
RACHEL LATENDRESSE
JOSHUA LATENDRESSE
SHALEENA RUSSELL
TERRI LATENDRESSE
JASON LATENDRESSE

Table Six
NATHAN BLEDSOE
HEIDI BLEDSOE
SHAWN KEARNEY
HEIDI KEARNEY
TINNA LEE
SIMON LEE

Table Seven
SUE HAWKINSON
BOB HAWKINSON
ALEX HAWKINSON
JESSICA HAWKINSON

Table Eight
TAMMY DOUGLAS
BOB DOUGLAS
HILARY DOUGLAS
ASHLEY DOUGLAS
ABBEY DOUGLAS
TONY McGOUGH

Table Nine
SAMANTHA SNYDER
BETTYJANE SNYDER
KEITH SNYDER
CASSANDRA SNYDER
EVERETTE ADAMS
JOANNE ORT
BROOKE REEVES
RYAN REEVES
EMILY KIM
VINCCI LAM

Table Ten
NATHAN KACH
CAROLYN KACH

ANDREW KLOESS
BRANDON WEBB
ARIANA DAWSON
MAX NAZARYAN
SEAN BROWN

MEGAN BROWN
CHARLOTTE BARILLEAUX
JEFF MUSHEN
GRANT HANSEN

This formal, modern, and urban wedding was held in downtown Seattle. The couple wanted to give their guests a pleasant and memorable experience, so they focused their budget on the venue, food, drinks, and music. The wedding had three major DIY projects: the save-the-dates, the centerpieces, and 1,000 folded paper cranes, which served as the backdrop of the head table. The save-the-dates were little boxes filled with champagne flavored candy, stamped with a custom stamp made from Antiquaria, and wrapped with a miniature black bow tie which was consistent with the wedding's black and gold palette.

BRIANNE & ERIK'S
SEATTLE ART GALLERY WEDDING

Artistic; Colorful; Geometric

Photographer
Carina Skrobecki

Designer/Studio
Brianne Tomlin (The bride)

Website
www.carinaskrobecki.com

Seattle, WA, USA

Confetti Bar!

1. Grab an envelope

2. Mix up a custom batch of confetti
to suit your style

3. Toss to celebrate the newlyweds
as they walk down the aisle

This wedding was a celebration of the culmination of a long engagement and a long distance relationship, therefore, it was important to the couple that the wedding should be an experience full of joy, happiness, and laughter for their close friends and family. This was translated by the use of bright colors, large bold patterns, and geometrical shapes—a nod to the groom's hobby of origami—and in an industrial venue to represent the bride's job as an architect. The celebration was adorned by thousands of hand-folded paper flowers, confetti, and patterns created by Tammie Bennet, to symbolize their bold and playful nature.

GERARD & CLARA'S WEDDING
Rustic

Photographer **Designer/Studio** **Website**
Magali Gómez Clara Roma Novellas www.clararoma.com

Catalonia, Spain

INSTAGRAM #gerardiclara

This is a rustic and romantic wedding celebrated in the countryside of forest and grasslands. The idyllic location transformed the simple wedding into an incredible party with a very natural touch fulfilling the expectation of the young couple. Guests and the newlyweds spent two days in a rural cottage to celebrate the wedding, so the couple wanted it to be casual, dynamic, fun, and fresh. To this end, a shaft section had been chosen as the backbone—manual typography with wooden stamp to convey proximity and a handmade touch.

A CANADIAN FALL WEDDING

Organic; Elegant

Photographer
Ameris Photography

Designer/Studio
Clare Day

Website
www.claredayflowers.ca

Villa Marco Polo, Victoria, BC, Canada

This is a celebration of love with romantic candlelight and rustic elements. The whole set of decorations toned in perfectly with the warm, breezy days of fall in the Pacific Northwest of Canada. Fall colours like blush and bronze, and refined details like the dresses and vintage candleholders combined with gorgeous local elements like cafe au lait dahlias, pears and beeswax candles helped create a romantic, elegant atmosphere for the wedding.

VICTORIA & KIERON'S
NOSTALGIC LOS ANGELES WEDDING
Vintage; Rustic

Photographer
Sarah Morrison of Hazelwood Photo

Designer/Studio
Party and Be Married

Website
www.hazelwoodphoto.com

Los Angeles, USA

This was a lovely wedding decorated with vintage elements where the couple focused more on aesthetics than on a solid wedding theme. They incorporated some of their favorite things in every detail in the wedding. The color scheme reflected the colors they like: ivory, gold, emeralds and metallic. With a love for vintage style, the bride chose a vintage dress that went well with the wedding palette. The bride and groom both collect vinyl records, so they used a DJ who spun vinyl and used old records for their seating charts. The wedding was held in the house where the bride grew up in, making family a major focus of the ceremony.

ELIZABETH & PRESTON'S
HIP NEW YORK FARM WEDDING

Pastoral; DIY

Photographer
Heidi Benjamin

Designer/Studio
Elizabeth Olson (The bride)

Website
www.heidibenjamin.com

NY, USA

HERE'S TO
HEALTH, WEALTH
&
HAPPINESS

JULY 27 2013

TABLE
TWO

With a love for design and a focus on details, the couple hand-crafted their entire wedding day, DIYing literally every aspect of the day. The wedding was held in a farm where natural elements played an important role in the venue decorations. From the balloon lined aisle to the rainbow inspired escort display to the hand sewn vintage daily table runners, this wedding included so many incredibly fun elements that were sure to inspire who are planning to hand make celebrations.

HELEN & STEVE'S WEDDING

Rustic; Typography Based

Photographer
Louise Hall & Sam Roberts

Designer/Studio
Bridges and Eggs Studio

Website
www.helenvbridges.co.uk

England, UK

This was an informal country wedding with delicious food, great music and nothing too conventional. The venue was on a farm in a barn in the middle of nowhere, with a tractor, straw bales, and wheat fields as a backdrop. The venue was decorated with screen printed signs, drawn chalk boards and an origami crane sculpture. The couple created their own unique rustic wedding stationery. They designed and screen printed a concertina invitation with attached RSVP to cut off and return, envelopes with their pig logo, matching the thank-you cards, menus, and message tags.

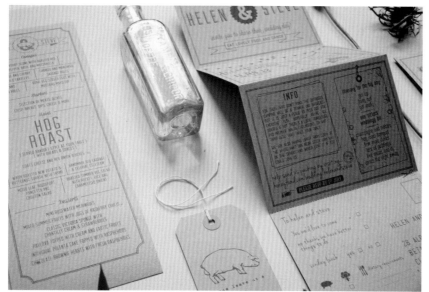

JOSHUA TREE WEDDING

Nature & Desert; DIY

Photographer
Martin Vielma

Designer/Studio
Hello Gem Events

Website
www.hellogem.com

Joshua Tree, CA, USA

1
YVONNE

11-17

T & R

JOSHUA TREE, CA

Gems and
Jewelry

WELCOME!

MANY THANKS FOR MAKING IT
OUT TO CELEBRATE WITH US

PLEASE FIND YOUR TABLE
NUMBER AND CHOOSE ANY SEAT
AT THAT TABLE

FOR THE CEREMONY, WE WOULD
LIKE YOU TO GATHER NEAR THE
REFLECTING POOL

OOD AND DRINKS WILL BE
BLE SHORTLY AFTER THE
CEREMONY

R STARTS AT 6:15

SURE TO LEAVE
UR GUEST BOOK

The couple wanted a comfortable and unique event that incorporated the natural beauty of the surrounding desert in California. Rocks and ropes were used as the main decoration throughout the space, combined with numbers of desert plants like succulents. The macramé garland hung over the dinner tables were created together with the bride, an art teacher, and her students.

OREGON SUMMER WEDDING

DIY; Pastoral

Photographer
Maria Lamb Photography

Designer/Studio
The Newlyweds & Their Family & Friends

Website
www.marialamb.co

OR, USA

SWANSON RESIDENCE

together with our parents, we

Hunter Paolo
&
Justin Abel

invite you to join in the celebration
of our marriage

THE SWANSON RESIDENCE
JULY 26, 2013
7:00 PM

You are welcome to
be our guests as we are wed
in a private ceremony

THE SWANSON RESIDENCE
July 26, 2013
5:56pm

With the couple's love for nostalgia, the DIY wedding was decorated with rustic and antique details that told their story. Their wedding took place in Damascus, Oregon on the bride's grandparents' property. Because the bride had spent a lot of time there growing up, it was very special that she could cherish some of her best memories from her wedding there. The reception area was decorated with strung lights and fabric draped in trees, the beverage and cake tables, and other details. The ceremony was in a forested pasture, and the bride's brother built an arbor of branches from the forest that they decorated with olive leaves and white roses for the wedding day.

Brent & Cathy's Wedding
Whimsical; DIY

Photographer
Visual Storytelling by Jonathan Ong

Designer/Studio
The Couple's Family & Friends

Website
www.jonathanong.com

Gippsland, Vic, Australia

This was a wedding filled with festive music and colors based on a teal, pink, yellow palette. Details in twine and paper, with paper aeroplanes used throughout the decorations and stationery made a lovely heart-warming DIY wedding. Colored flags in different sizes were hung above the backyard, where the wedding was held. The warm palette, along with the beautiful sunlight added to the joy of the couple.

Jenny & Nick's Wedding
Whimsical; DIY

Photographer
Red White and Green Photography

Designer/Studio
Muse and Delphia

Website
redwhiteandgreen.squarespace.com

Charlotte, NC, USA

This was a fun and light-hearted yet still a little sentimental wedding with an umbrella candy shower ceremony. The bride picked the "Love is Weird" theme because she knew it would justify her basically just throwing together things she liked for the decor. She viewed the day as a time of immense joy and happiness. Everything was kept to be beautifully simple. The bride created the table markers by spray painting unique porcelain figurines. Place cards were made with the silhouette of creature of each guest's corresponding table.

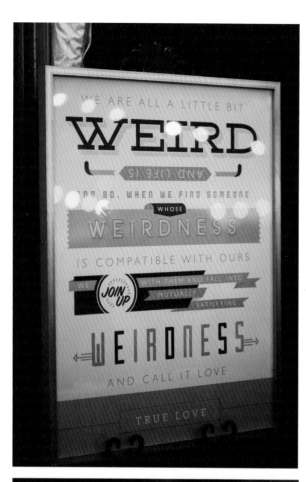

WE ARE ALL A LITTLE BIT
WEIRD
— AND LIFE IS —
TOO SO, WHEN WE FIND SOMEONE
WHOSE
WEIRDNESS
IS COMPATIBLE WITH OURS
WE **JOIN UP** WITH THEM AND FALL INTO
MUTUALLY SATISFYING
WEIRDNESS
→ AND CALL IT LOVE ←

TRUE LOVE

Jaymee & Reis's wedding

Beach; DIY

Photographer
Annie McElwain

Designer/Studio
Jaymee Harney (The bride)

Website
www.jayadores.com

Santa Barbara, CA, USA

Miss Jaymee Zeller
5815 Pukalani Place
Honolulu, Hawaii
9 . 6 . 8 . 1 . 6

PRETTY PLEASE
Rsvp
NO LATER THAN OCTOBER 13TH

PLEASE CHECK ONE

SUNDAY
NOVEMBER
ELEVENTH
TWO THOUSAND TWELVE
THREE O'CLOCK
IN THE AFTERNOON

Jaymee
Nicole
Reis
Thomas
TO

RANCHO
DOS
PUEBLOS
SANTA BARBARA
CALIFORNIA

ACCOMMODATIONS
PARKING/SHUTTLE INFORMATION
THINGS TO DO IN SANTA BARBARA
REGISTRY

THE DETAILS

JAYMEE AND REIS ARE GETTING
MARRIED TODAY

GOURMET KETTLE CORN

RYAN BEYER | 11

KALVI BERRY / GROOMSMAN

This was a DIY beach wedding characterized by bluffs, woods, and a rustic barn. The ceremony was held on the bluffs with a spectacular view overlooking the ocean while the reception was in a barn with a rustic exterior. To create a contrast, the interior of the barn was decorated to be classy and modern with a vintage twist. Meanwhile, the initials of the couple were added to the back of the barn, creating a focal point which could be seen when guests entered the barn. As for the other details, since the bride was keen to "brand" their wedding, most of the decorations were designed by the couple themselves, such as a logo, the invitations, menus, welcome boxes, signage, newspapers and coffee bag favors. Every small detail was made cohesive and helped set the tone for the big day.

Nathanael & Shannon Clanton's Wedding

Rustic; Elegant

Photographer
Bethany Small Photography

Designer/Studio
The Couple & Their Family & Friends

Website
www.bethanysmall.com

Beaverton, OR, USA

choose a seat
not a side
we're all family
once the knot
is tied

Nathaniel
&
5·30·2014
Shannon

The beautiful open field with leafy trees set a rustic and elegant vibe for the wedding. As perfect as planned, the wedding day was characterized by golden sunshine, children playing, tons of laughter, and a giant celebration filled with light, textures and sounds. It was not so much a wedding as a giant whimsical party full of people the new couple love for people created the wonderful event together by contributing their time and efforts and celebrated closely. The horses, the groom's favorite animal, added more joy to the day.

CATHERINE & ROBERT'S WEDDING
Garden Party

Photographer
Craig & Eva Sanders Photography

Designer/Studio
Catherine Cole of Peonie Cole

Website
www.craigevasanders.co.uk

Ayrshire, Scotland, UK

This couple wanted the wedding to have a garden party theme with hints of their Parisian engagement, lace details and lots of seasonal country-style flowers including peonies and hydrangeas. They married in June since the venue would be filled with rhododendrons at that time, which completed the garden party theme. Pink, the bride's favorite color, and blue, the gloom's favored one, were perfectly incorporated and set the tone for the whole wedding.

Fresh flowers in shades of coral, blush pink, white and light blue were used to create a garden party vibe. A lot of the wedding decoration items were printed with beautiful floral designed by the bride to match the theme as well, including the handmade fabric pouches for bridesmaids with their initials and printed pocket mirrors for guests. Fairy lights, meters of bunting and tissue paper pompoms in pinks and blues were used to decorate the reception place, creating a romantic atmosphere. Small bunches of flowers and table number details emphasized the floral theme.

ding

ments

Contents
Wedding Elements

P196 / P219 / P243 / P252
The Daphne Wedding Cake
Photographer: Sharida Moore
Designer/Studio: Artisan Cakes of Atlanta
Website: www.artisancakesofatl.com

P197
Dian & Wicak's Wedding
Designer/Studio: Diasty Hardhikaputri
Website: www.behance.net/hardhikaputri

P197 / P241 / P245 / P248 / P251
The Artist and the Scientist
Photographer: Page Bertelsen
Designer/Studio: Honey & Twine Weddings and Events
Website: www.honeyandtwine.com

P198
Cristina & David's Wedding
Photographer: El Calotipo Printing Studio
Designer/Studio: El Calotipo Printing Studio
Website: www.elcalotipo.com

P198
Clara & Daniel's Wedding
Photographer: El Calotipo Printing Studio
Designer/Studio: El Calotipo Printing Studio
Website: www.elcalotipo.com

P198 / P212
Jenna & Brian's Wedding
Photographer: Chelsea Davis
Designer/Studio: Atheneum Creative
Website: www.atheneumcreative.com

P199
A Brand for Tomas and Teresa's Wedding
Photographer: Gianluca & Mary Adovasio
Designer/Studio: Concreate Studio
Website: www.concreate.it

P199
Laurie and Jaime Oesterle's Wedding
Designer/Studio: Andrea Sturgell
Website: www.chirp-paperie.com

P200
Elo & Fer's Wedding
Photographer: El Calotipo Printing Studio
Designer/Studio: El Calotipo Printing Studio
Website: www.elcalotipo.com

P200
Daniel and Tabitha's Wedding
Photographer: Luisa Brimble
Designer/Studio: Tabitha Emma
Website: tabithaemma.com

P201
Agnieszka Rogatty & Szymon Grykier's Wedding
Photographer: Zuzanna Rogatty
Designer/Studio: Zuzanna Rogatty
Website: www.behance.net/rogatty

P201
A Moscow Wedding
Photographer: Roman Suvorov
Designer/Studio: Anya Aleksandrova
Website: www.anya-aleksandrova.com

P201 / P233 / P249
Stephanie & Mikael's Sweden Park Wedding
Photographer: Therese Winberg Photography
Designer/Studio: Stephanie Wänersten
Website: www.theresewinberg.com

P201 / P211 / P213 / P215 / P217
Greg & Jenny's Wedding
Photographer: Therese Aherne
Website: www.thereseaherneweddings.com

P201 / P213 / P222 / P232 / P237 / P243 / P251
Grace and Michael's Wedding
Photographer: Andrew Mark Photography
Designer/Studio: Ashley Lindzon Design
Website: www.andrewmark.ca

P201 / P218 / P229 / P233 / P236 / P252
Summer Lemonade Stand Wedding Inspiration
Photographer: Sandy Tam Photography
Designer/Studio: Berlyn Lai from Bloved Events
Website: sandytam.ca

P201 / P246 / P248
We Are One
Photographer: Gary Didsbury
Designer/Studio: Knot & Pop
Website: www.knotandpop.com

P202 / P218 / P232 / P240 / P243
Heirloom Wedding Ideas
Photographer: Katie Stoops Photography
Designer/Studio: Momental Designs
Website: www.momentaldesigns.com

P204
Joe and Bee's Wedding Suite
Designer/Studio: Belinda Love Lee
Website: belindalovelee.com

P204 / P222 / P241 / P251
Waiting for My Sailor
Designer/Studio: Roberto Monaldi
Photographer: Cinzia Bruschini
Stationary Designer: Shhh My Darling
Website: robertomonaldi.com

P205
French Garden Party Wedding Invitations
Photographer: Coral Pheasant
Designer/Studio: Coral Pheasant Stationery
Website: www.coralpheasant.com

P205
Dimitri & Elena's Wedding
Photographer: Martina Zancan
Designer/Studio: Dry Design
Website: www.dry-design.it

P206
Lucy and Stefan Marek's Wedding
Photographer: Rebecca Li
Designer/Studio: Theresa Ptak
Website: theresaptak.com

P206 / P211 / P212 / P249
Lindsey & Sean's Industrial Brooklyn Wedding
Photographer: Therese Winberg Photography
Website: www.theresewinberg.com

P206 / P212 / P222 / P227 / P228 / P234 / P237 / P238 / P249
Outi & Masa's Finland Archipelago Boho Wedding
Photographer: Therese Winberg Photography
Designer/Studio: Outi Mäkinen
Website: www.theresewinberg.com

P206 / P217 / P234 / P246 / P248
Dark Romantic
Photographer: Heather Waraska
Designer/Studio: Clara Chic Weddings
Website: www.chicweddingsinitaly.com

P206 / P229 / P234 / P237 / P247 / P249 / P253
Susie & Moss' Scotland Wedding
Photographer: Ed Peers Photography
Designer/Studio: Knot & Pop
Website: www.edpeers.com

P207
Zsófi and Bálint's Wedding
Photographer: Eszter Laki
Designer/Studio: Eszter Laki
Website: behance.net/lakieszti

P207 / P210 / P212 / P214 / P217 / P239 / P249 / P252
Lynn & Richard's Sweden Woodland Wedding
Photographer: Therese Winberg Photography
Designer/Studio: Lynn Kullman
Website: www.theresewinberg.com

P207 / P244 / P249
French Country Shoot
Photographer: Rebecca Hollis Photography
Designer/Studio: Alisa Lewis Event Design
Website: alisa-Lewis.com

P208
US Project
Photographer: Convictus
Designer/Studio: Convictus
Website: www.convictus.pt

P208
Júlia & Ricardo's Wedding
Photographer: Convictus
Designer/Studio: Convictus
Website: www.convictus.pt

P209
Susana & Pedro's Wedding
Photographer: Convictus
Designer/Studio: Convictus
Website: www.convictus.pt

P209
Diana & Guilherme's Wedding
Photographer: Convictus
Designer/Studio: Convictus
Website: www.convictus.pt

P211 / P212 / P227 / P233 / P246
Diane & Julien's Normandy Summer Wedding
Photographer: Studio A+Q
Website: www.studioaq.com

P211 / P219 / P232 / P235 / P237
Mandy & Dylan's Wedding
Photographer: Nikita Lee Photography
Website: www.nikitalee.com

P211 / P224 / P227 / P233 / P235 / P237 / P238 / P239
Karen & Kevin's Wedding
Photographer: Heidi Lau Photography
Website: www.heidilau.ca

P211 / P236 / P249
Organic Tablescape Shoot
Photographer: Urban Rose Photo
Designer/Studio: Alisa Lewis Event Design
Website: alisa-Lewis.com

P212 / P213 / P225
Nathanael & Shannon's Wedding
Photographer: Bethany Small Photography
Website: www.bethanysmall.com

P213
Silver Anniversary
Designer/Studio: Silver Wedding
Website: silverwedding.com.cn

P214 / P219 / P231 / P235 / P238 / P243 / P250
Jenna & Rob's Wedding
Photographer: Simply Bloom Photography, LLC
Website: simplybloomphotography.com

P217
Gambling-themed Wedding
Designer/Studio: Silver Wedding
Website: silverwedding.com.cn

P216 / P229 / P230 / P234 / P253
Jen & Cody's Wedding
Photographer: Simply Bloom Photography, LLC
Website: simplybloomphotography.com

P218
Text Cake
Photographer: Lovely Cakes
Designer/Studio: Lovely Cakes
Website: www.lovelycakes.net

P218
Yellow Cake
Photographer: Lovely Cakes
Designer/Studio: Lovely Cakes
Website: www.lovelycakes.net

P219
Libbie & Jesse's Napa Valley Wedding
Photographer: The Wedding Artists Collective
Designer/Studio: Jubilee Lau Events &
                 Gloria Wong Design
Website: www.theweddingac.com

P220 / P221
Five Wedding Cakes
Designer/Studio: Baked In Caked Out
Website: www.bakedincakedout.com

P223 / P233 / P238 / P239 / P247 / P252
Lindsay & Eoin's Pastel Picnic Wedding
Photographer: Ewa Figaszewska Photography
Website: www.weddingsindublin.com

P226
Oregon Summer Wedding
Photographer: Maria Lamb Photography
Website: www.marialamb.co

P227
Catherine & Robert's Wedding
Photographer: Craig & Eva Sanders Photography
Website: www.craigevasanders.co.uk

P227
Heritage Woodland Oak Grove Wedding
Photographer: Let's Frolic Together
Website: www.letsfrolictogether.com

P228 / P233 / P235 / P237
Love in the Fall
Photographer: Liuzai Wedding Photography
Designer/Studio: Real Wedding Planning Studio
Website: weibo.com/u/2629103357

P228 / P240
The 1950s American Vintage Wedding Party
Photographer: Yan Min
Designer/Studio: IMAGINE WEDDING
Website: www.imaginegroup.cn

P229
Love is the Color Blue
Photographer: Captain Photography Studio
Designer/Studio: B.loved Wedding
Website: www.b-loved.cn

P229
Shangri-La Wedding
Designer/Studio: Silver Wedding
Website: silverwedding.com.cn

P232 / P237 / P246 / P248
Farm Shoot Ceremony
Photographer: Bryan N. Miller Photography
Designer/Studio: Wedding Elegance by Nahid
Website: www.weddingelegancesd.com

P232 / P240
The Wizard of Oz
Photographer: Ethan & Lin He
Designer/Studio: IMAGINE WEDDING
Website: www.imaginegroup.cn

P234
Jenny and Nick's Wedding
Photographer: Red White and Green Photography
Designer/Studio: Muse and Delphia
Website: redwhiteandgreen.squarespace.com

P239
Jaymee and Reis's Wedding
Photographer: Annie McElwain
Designer/Studio: Jaymee Harney
Website: www.jayadores.com

P242 / P248
Tablescape Shoot
Photographer: Milou + Olin Photography
Designer/Studio: Caroline Winata and Very Merry Events
Website: www.milouandolin.com

©Libbie & Jesse's Napa Valley Wedding

©Dian & Wicak's Wedding

©The Artist and the Scientist

©Cristina & David's Wedding

©Clara & Daniel's Wedding

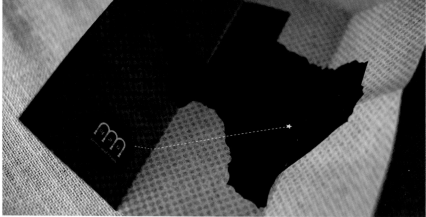

©A Brand for Tomas and Teresa's Wedding

©Laurie and Jaime Oesterle's Wedding

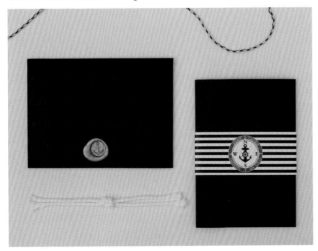

©Elo & Fer's Wedding

©Daniel and Tabitha's Wedding

©Agnieszka Rogatty & Szymon Grykier's Wedding

©We Are One

©Greg & Jenny's Wedding

©Grace and Michael's Wedding

©A Moscow Wedding

©Summer Lemonade Stand Wedding Inspiration

©Stephanie & Mikael's Sweden Park Wedding

we shall dine

and revel in the day's joys

ONE

VICHYSSOISE *with* LEMON OIL

TWO

CITRUS AND HEIRLOOM TOMATO SALAD
WITH PINK PEPPERCORNS

THREE

TRIO OF TEA SANDWHICHES

FOUR

INDIVIDUAL VEGETABLE TERRINE
WITH GRILLED BREADS

©Waiting for My Sailor

©Joe and Bee's Wedding Suite

©French Garden Party Wedding Invitations

©Dimitri & Elena's Wedding

©Lucy and Stefan Marek's Wedding

© Dark Romantic

©Outi & Masa's Finland Archipelago Boho Wedding

©Lindsey & Sean's Industrial Brooklyn Wedding

©Susie & Moss' Scotland Wedding

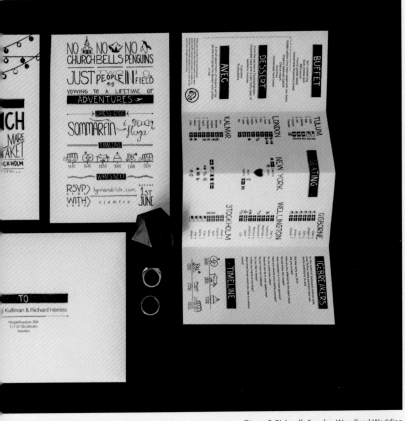

©Lynn & Richard's Sweden Woodland Wedding

©Zsófi and Bálint's Wedding

©French Country Shoot

©Susana & Pedro's Wedding

©Diana & Guilherme's Wedding

©Lindsey & Sean's Industrial
Brooklyn Wedding

©Karen & Kevin's Wedding

©Diane & Julien's Normandy Summer Wedding

©Greg & Jenny's Wedding

©Mandy & Dylan's Wedding

©Organic Tablescape Shoot

Reception

©Diane & Julien's Normandy Summer Wedding

©Outi & Masa's Finland Archipelago Boho Wedding

©Jenna & Brian's Wedding

©Lynn & Richard's Sweden Woodland Wedding

©Lindsey & Sean's Industrial Brooklyn Wedding

©Nathanael & Shannon's Wedding

©Silver Anniversary

©Greg & Jenny's Wedding

©Grace and Michael's Wedding

©Nathanael & Shannon's Wedding

©Jenna & Rob's Wedding

©Lynn & Richard's Sweden Woodland Wedding

©Greg & Jenny's Wedding

Cakes

©Lynn & Richard's Sweden Woodland Wedding

©Dark Romantic

©Gambling-themed Wedding

©Greg & Jenny's Wedding

©Text Cake

©Yellow Cake

©Summer Lemonade Stand Wedding Inspiration

©Heirloom Wedding Ideas

©The Daphne Wedding Cake

©Libbie & Jesse's Napa Valley Wedding

©Jenna & Rob's Wedding

©Mandy & Dylan's Wedding

©Five Wedding Cakes

©Waiting for My Sailor

©Outi & Masa's Finland Archipelago Boho Wedding

©Grace and Michael's Wedding

©Lindsay & Eoin's Pastel Picnic Wedding

©Karen & Kevin's Wedding

©Outi & Masa's Finland Archipelago Boho Wedding

©Catherine & Robert's Wedding

©Heritage Woodland Oak Grove Wedding

©Diane & Julien's Normandy Summer Wedding

©Karen & Kevin's Wedding

©The 1950s American Vintage Wedding Party

©Outi & Masa's Finland Archipelago Boho Wedding

©Love in the Fall

©Susie & Moss' Scotland Wedding

©Love is the Color Blue

©Shangri-La Wedding

©Summer Lemonade Stand Wedding Inspiration

©Jen & Cody's Wedding

Floral Decoration

©Jenna & Rob's Wedding

©The Wizard of Oz

©Heirloom Wedding Ideas

©Grace and Michael's Wedding

©Farm Shoot Ceremony

©Mandy & Dylan's Wedding

©Love in the Fall

©Diane & Julien's Normandy Summer Wedding

©Karen & Kevin's Wedding

©Stephanie & Mikael's Sweden Park Wedding

©Lindsay & Eoin's Pastel Picnic Wedding

©Summer Lemonade Stand Wedding Inspiration

©Dark Romantic

©Outi & Masa's Finland Archipelago Boho Wedding

©Jenny and Nick's Wedding

©Susie & Moss' Scotland Wedding

©Jen & Cody's Wedding

©Mandy & Dylan's Wedding

©Love in the Fall

©Karen & Kevin's Wedding

©Jenna & Rob's Wedding

©Karen & Kevin's Wedding

©Organic Tablescape Shoot

©Summer Lemonade Stand Wedding Inspiration

©Farm Shoot Ceremony

©Grace and Michael's Wedding

©Love in the Fall

©Karen & Kevin's Wedding

©Susie & Moss' Scotland Wedding

©Mandy & Dylan's Wedding

©Outi & Masa's Finland Archipelago Boho Wedding

©Karen & Kevin's Wedding

©Lindsay & Eoin's Pastel Picnic Wedding

©Jenna & Rob's Wedding

©Outi & Masa's Finland Archipelago Boho Wedding

©Lynn & Richard's Sweden Woodland Wedding

©Jaymee and Reis's wedding

©Karen & Kevin's Wedding

©Lindsay & Eoin's Pastel Picnic Wedding

©Heirloom Wedding Ideas

©The Wizard of Oz

©The 1950s American Vintage Wedding Party

©The 1950s American Vintage Wedding Party

Tablescape

©Jenna & Rob's Wedding

©Heirloom Wedding Ideas

©Libbie & Jesse's Napa Valley Wedding

©Grace and Michael's Wedding

©French Country Shoot

©The Artist and the Scientist

©Farm Shoot Ceremony

©Diane & Julien's Normandy Summer Wedding

©Dark Romantic

©We Are One

©Lindsay & Eoin's Pastel Picnic Wedding

©Susie & Moss' Scotland Wedding

©Dark Romantic

©The Artist and the Scientist

©We Are One

©Farm Shoot Ceremony

©Tablescape Shoot

©French Country Shoot

©Organic Tablescape Shoot

©Stephanie & Mikael's Sweden Park Wedding

©Outi & Masa's Finland Archipelago Boho Wedding

©Lynn & Richard's Sweden Woodland Wedding

©Lindsey & Sean's Industrial Brooklyn Wedding

©Susie & Moss' Scotland Wedding

Decoration

©Grace and Michael's Wedding

©The Artist and the Scientist

©Waiting for My Sailor

©Libbie & Jesse's Napa Valley Wedding

©Lynn & Richard's Sweden Woodland Wedding

©Summer Lemonade Stand Wedding Inspiration

©Lindsay & Eoin's Pastel Picnic Wedding

©Susie & Moss' Scotland Wedding

©Jen & Cody's Wedding

Index

Alisa Lewis Event Design
alisa-Lewis.com
P207 / P211 / P236 / P244 / P249

Andrea Sturgell
www.chirp-paperie.com
P199

Andrew Mark Photography
www.andrewmark.ca
P201 / P213 / P222 / P232 / P237 /P243 / P251

Anthem Photography
www.anthemphotography.com
P226

Anya Aleksandrova
www.anya-aleksandrova.com
P201

Artisan Cakes of Atlanta
www.artisancakesofatl.com
P219

Atheneum Creative
www.atheneumcreative.com
P198 / P212

B.loved Wedding
www.b-loved.cn
P229

Baked In Caked Out
www.bakedincakedout.com
P220 / P221

Belinda Love Lee
belindalovelee.com
P204

Bethany Small Photography
www.bethanysmall.com
P176 / P212 / P213 / P225

Bridges and Eggs Studio
www.helenvbridges.co.uk
P138

Carina Skrobecki
www.carinaskrobecki.com
P94 / P102 / P108

Clara Chic Weddings
www.chicweddingsinitaly.com
P206 / P217 / P234 / P246 / P248

Clara Roma Novellas
www.clararoma.com
P114

Clare Day
www.claredayflowers.ca
P120

Concreate Studio
www.concreate.it
P72 / P199

Convictus
www.convictus.pt
P208 / P209

Coral Pheasant Stationery
www.coralpheasant.com
P205

Craig & Eva Sanders Photography
www.craigevasanders.co.uk
P186 / P227

Danielle Poff Photography
www.daniellepoff.com
P82

Diasty Hardhikaputri
www.behance.net/hardhikaputri
P197

Dry Design
www.dry-design.it
P205

Ed Peers Photography
www.edpeers.com
P206 / P229 / P234 / P237 / P247 / P249 / P253

El Calotipo Printing Studio
www.elcalotipo.com
P198 / P200

Eszter Laki
behance.net/lakieszti
P207

Ewa Figaszewska Photography
www.weddingsindublin.com
P223 / P233 / P238 / P239 / P247 / P252

Heidi Benjamin
www.heidibenjamin.com
P132

Heidi Lau Photography
www.heidilau.ca
P211 / P224 / P227 / P233 / P235 / P237 /P238 / P239

Hello Gem Events
www.hellogem.com
P144

Honey & Twine Weddings and Events
www.honeyandtwine.com
P197 / P241 / P245 / P248 / P251

IMAGINE WEDDING
www.imaginegroup.cn
P88 / P228 / P232 / P240

Jaymee Harney
www.jayadores.com
P170 / P239

Knot & Pop
www.knotandpop.com
P201 / P246 / P248

Lad & Lass Wedding Photography
www.ladandlass.co.za
P44

Let's Frolic Together
www.letsfrolictogether.com
P22 / P227

Lovely Cakes
www.lovelycakes.net
P218

Mandy Forlenza Sticos
mandyforlenza.com
P50

Maria Lamb Photography
www.marialamb.co
P150 / P226

Milou + Olin Photography
milouandolin.com
P78 / P242 / P248

Momental Designs
www.momentaldesigns.com
P202 / P218 / P232 / P240 / P243

Nadia Huerta
junebugcompany.com
P12 / P56

Nikita Lee Photography
www.nikitalee.com
P211 / P219 / P232 / P235 / P237

Real Wedding Planning Studio
weibo.com/u/2629103357
P228 / P233 / P235 / P237

Red White and Green Photography
redwhiteandgreen.squarespace.com
P164 / P234

Roberto Monaldi
robertomonaldi.com
P204 / P222 / P241 / P251

Sandy Tam Photography
sandytam.ca
P201 / P218 / P229 / P233 / P236 / P252

Sarah Morrison of Hazelwood Photo
www.hazelwoodphoto.com
P126

Silver Wedding
silverwedding.com.cn
P213 / P217 / P229

Simply Bloom Photography, LLC
simplybloomphotography.com
P214 / P216 / P219 / P229 / P230 / P231 /
P234 /P235 / P238 / P243 / P250 / P253

Simply Loves Wedding & Design
simplyloves.com
P18

Studio A+Q
www.studioaq.com
P211 / P212 / P227 / P233 / P246

Swan Real Wedding
www.wedding-swan.com
P38

Tabitha Emma
tabithaemma.com
P200

Taylor Made Events and Design
www.taylormadeeventsanddesign.com
P28

The Wedding Artists Collective
www.theweddingac.com
P196 / P219 / P243 / P252

Theresa Ptak
theresaptak.com
P206

Therese Aherne
www.thereseaherneweddings.com
P201 / P211 / P213 / P215 / P217

Therese Winberg Photography
www.theresewinberg.com
P201 / P206 / P207 / P210 / P211 / P212 /
P214 / P217 / P222 / P227 / P228 / P233 /
P234 / P237 / P238 / P239 / P249 / P252

Thomas Steibl
www.thomassteibl.com
P62

Tiffany Bowne of Lounge Couture Inc.
www.loungecouture.com
P66

TOGETHER
weibo.com/u/3234496314?topnav=1&wvr=
6&topsug=1
P34

Visual Storytelling by Jonathan Ong
www.jonathanong.com
P156

Wedding Elegance by Nahid
www.weddingelegancesd.com
P232 / P237 / P246 / P248

Zuzanna Rogatty
www.behance.net/rogatty
P201

Acknowledgements

We would like to thank all the designers and contributers who have been involved in the production of this book. Their contribution is indispensable in the compilation of this book. We would also like to express our gratitude to all the producers for their invaluable opinions and assistance throughout this project. And to the many others whose names are not credited but have aided in the production of this book, we thank you for your continuous support.